A

ACARAJÉ: This recipe for stuffed black-eyed pea fritters was brought to Salvador (Brazil) by African immigrants. It is used in the rituals of the local religious tradition Candomblé, and most of its female practitioners are also acarajé street vendors. It is still widely eaten in west Africa.

BURRITO: On the difference between a burrito and a taco: tacos are made with warmed corn tortillas which are simply folded over, whereas burritos, a more recent invention, are made with wheat tortillas, wrapped to form a tight parcel.

C

CHURROS: Traditionally eaten in the early morning of New Year's Day in Spain, these doughnut-like treats are rolled in sugar and then dipped in chocolate or coffee. The thicker, larger variant is called 'porra'.

D

DANGO: An old Japanese proverb goes 'hana yori dango' which literally means 'dumplings before flowers' – one should take the practical over the aesthetic.

E

EMPANADA: A stuffed pastry, baked or fried, common in parts of southern Europe and most of Latin America. The name comes from the Portuguese and Spanish verb 'empanar', meaning to wrap in bread. The original idea consisted of filling bread with meat or vegetables so that shepherds and travellers could eat them on journeys. The same principle can be seen in Italian calzone and Cornish pasties.

FISH AND CHIPS: Weirdly enough, the chip may have been invented as a substitute for fish, rather than an accompaniment. According to popular history, when the rivers froze over and nothing could be caught, resourceful British housewives cut potatoes into fish shapes and fried them instead. During World War II, the UK government made sure fish and chips was one of the few foods exempt from rationing.

G

GYROS: From the Greek word for 'turn', gyros are made from meat roasted on a vertical rotating spit. In Greece and Cyprus the meat used is typically pork or chicken. 'Turn' in Turkish is 'döner', and a döner kebab is similar, except that lamb, beef or chicken are used. In Arabic-speaking countries and Israel, a similar dish is called 'shawarma'. In France, this popular fast food is sold as 'sandwich grec' (Greek sandwich).

H

HOT DOG: Though we can't be sure whether he came up with the term himself, research points to the original 'hot dog man' being a Jamaican-born, German-speaking former circus strongman at the end of the nineteenth century. As well as being nicknamed 'Hot Dog' Morris after peddling hot frankfurters in New Jersey, he was also known as 'Pepper Sauce' Morris after the popular sauce he invented.

I

ICE CREAM: During World War II the US Army set up ice-cream parlours near the front line, believing it to be important for the morale of the troops. Ice cream became such an American symbol that Mussolini banned it in Italy, the country that claims to have invented the world-renowned modern recipe. He then went on to lose the war...

JALEBI: One cannot conceive of a national holiday in India without the luscious and mouth-watering jalebis being sold on every street corner in sight. Though a very cheap sweet, the price soars by 50 per cent on such occasions due to extraordinary demand. It is also a very popular choice during Ramadan, especially in Pakistan.

K

KENKEY: This sourdough dumpling, served with stew or sauce, has deep roots in the culture of the Akan (the biggest ethnic group in Ghana and the Ivory Coast). In the famous Asante tales, one of the characters is called 'Half a Ball of Kenkey'.

LÁNGOS: A deep-fried flatbread often referred to as Hungarian pizza, the main difference is that the toppings go on the bread after it has been cooked. The most popular version is simply rubbed with garlic butter and topped with sour cream and grated cheese. Its name comes from 'láng', the Hungarian word for flame.

M

MERGUEZ: A thin, spicy sausage of North African origin now popular in France and the Middle East: traditionally made with lamb, merguez may also be prepared with beef, or a mixture of the two. Its characteristic red colour and distinct spicy flavour come from a combination of paprika, cayenne pepper, cumin, fennel and harissa.

N

NIEUWE HARING: Herring from the North Sea caught at the end of spring is stored in small containers ('vaatjes') and brought to shore. The first 'vaatje' to land is traditionally auctioned off and it makes headline news. To eat it the Dutch way, pick the raw herring up by the tail and let it slide into your mouth gradually – the head having been removed.

OTAK-OTAK: This Peranakan specialty is a delightful snack (and an acquired taste) consisting of fish paste mashed with coconut milk, garlic, lemongrass and chilli paste. It is wrapped in a steamed banana or pandan leaf and then grilled over a charcoal fire. 'Otak-otak' means brains in Malay, the name derived from its soft, mushy texture.

P

PRETZEL: Supposedly invented by monks to reward little children who had memorized their prayers, the pretzel's knotted symmetrical shape depicts the crossed arms of a child praying. The name may derive from the German 'brezel' or from 'pretiola', meaning 'little reward' in Latin.

Q

QASSATAT: Small ricotta, spinach, anchovy or pea pies, these tasty snacks have been part of Malta's food culture since the time of the Knights of St John and were traditionally baked for Easter.

R

RED-RED: A common Ghanaian stew named after the colour of its red palm oil and tomatoes. The red-red cowpea (or black-eyed pea) stew is usually served with fried plantains and is a lunch favourite in Ghana. If you are 'unbeanz', (unemployed) you can survive on this meal as the ingredients are inexpensive (cowpeas are indigenous to Africa).

S

STARFISH: How does one eat a starfish? You break off a leg and pry it open following the fissure in the middle, and then lick out the green goo inside, which is supposed to taste like crab brain or sea urchins, another delicacy.

T

TAMALES: Originally dating back over 3,000 years, stuffed corn-dough tamales were a staple for the Aztecs, Mayans and Incas and were heavily connected to mythology in pre-Hispanic America. According to legend, if you ate a tamale which had got stuck to the pan while cooking, you would never be able to shoot your arrows well...

U

UYKULUK: An Istanbul delicacy consisting of grilled lamb or calf sweetbreads seasoned with oregano and Aleppo pepper flakes. Sütlüce, also known as the sweetbreads district, is a neighbourhood of Istanbul on the Golden Horn where all the slaughterhouses were based half a century ago, and it is still reputedly the best place to go for uykuluk.

VATAPÁ: A seafood stew made from bread, shrimp, coconut milk and peanuts, this iconic Bahian dish is an integral part of the culture in that Brazilian state, appearing in song lyrics and even in Jorge Amado's novel 'Dona Flor and Her Two Husbands'.

W

WAFFLES: A crisp wafer became a honeycombed waffle in the thirteenth century when the iron plates used to press the wafers started being decorated with designs. The patterns included landscapes, coats of arms, religious motifs and the one that gave the waffle its current name, a honeycomb, from the Frankish word 'wafla'.

X

XA XIU: It literally means 'roasted on a fork' after the traditional cooking method: hanging strips of marinated boneless pork on skewers and roasting them in an oven or over a fire. Originally from south-eastern China, this dish is now a favourite all over Asia, called 'char siu' in Cantonese, 'cha shao' in Mandarin and 'xa xiu' in Vietnamese.

Y

YANG ROU CHUAN: Originally cooked by Chinese Muslims living in Xinjiang, western China, yang rou chuan is now arguably the most popular street food in the country. Essentially skewers of marinated lamb grilled over smouldering hot coals and served smoking off the grill, it can be found everywhere at almost any time of day and night. On summer evenings, groups of friends or family stand in front of roadside snack kiosks, having a plate of kebabs and a glass of cold beer.

Z

ZAPIEKANKA: A Polish open-faced baguette of epic dimensions. Zapiekanka's only essential ingredients are mushrooms and cheese, making it a low-cost meal, extremely popular with students. After being baked in the oven (more like a pizza than a sandwich), it is topped with ketchup or chives, with a beer as a perfect accompaniment. Na zdrowie!

Illustrations © 2014 Sophia Augusta
Design by Shaz Madani

Magma for Laurence King
www.laurenceking.com
ISBN: 978-1-85669-942-6